Letters to my imaginary wife

jp mackie

by E.M. Schorb

What the fortunate reader of *Letters to My Imaginary Wife* has in hand is a book-length, epistolary, narrative poem of great originality and sensitivity, and this reader deeply appreciates his visit to the magical terrain of James Mackie's mind. Caution: Do not let the title deceive you; *Letters* should not be thought of in terms of strophes, but as a whole, as a single, powerful narrative poem.

There is a strangeness about *Letters* that gives it mystery, always an ingredient of beauty, and beauty it has in abundance, and this strangeness resides in the fact that the poet's imaginary wife is also the poet, his Doppelgänger. But she is not his perfect double.

The imaginary wife – and it must be remembered that she is imaginary, an aspect of the poet – lives in the city and is worldly, filled with humanitarian instincts, and the desire to do good. The poet, on the other hand, the poet in the woods, is introverted, aerial, ethereal. He lives, emotionally, *sub specie aeternitatis*. She is Chaplin, the good hearted little tramp who always wants to make things better; he is Garbo, the embodiment of the beauty and mystery of life – and the miracle and the mystery of this poem is that they are both the poet, the poet wishing to make the world better and the poet wishing to be let alone with his thoughts.

This implicit dichotomy, and resultant conflict, keeps the tension high in a poem that might otherwise be static; but *Letters to My Imaginary Wife* is anything but static; it is a dynamic narrative, and a great gift from James Mackie to the world. If the world has any sense, or sensibility, it will value it highly.

~

E.M. Schorb's *Murderer's Day* was awarded the Verna Emery Poetry Prize and published by Purdue University Press. His novel, *Paradise Square*, won the Grand Prize for Fiction from the International eBook Award Foundation at the Frankfurt Book Fair.

~

LETTERS TO MY IMAGINARY WIFE:
AN ABSTRACT [5x2x6]

A book of letters troubling love entices
the dialogue.   Winds lisp   gentleness

through grass   around and over stone   almost
liquid   and rain in bubbled   crystal domes

wobble and sway on long grass blades quiver
in morning's freshest air   a taste   a sweet.

Is this the map   the dotted line   the once
illusive trail of bread crumbs tossed   to lead -

mislead enchanted souls?   A city's needs
have culled your passions   actions   hand and heart.

I sit and wait   as every fluttering leaf
amazes me   our story   unfolds   anew.

CR
... £etters ...

LOVE'S FIRST BREATH:
A LOVE SONNET FOR MY IMAGINARY WIFE

Start from death's slumber to eternity
Jones Very

The blue   the purest blue imaginable
Now fades along a staggered line of oak
And pine.   A mouth of wind   assembling sounds
In search of spirit   once an idle man
Noise oddly passed through bones   my bones
unthrilled
By sounds that start from death's slumber to
Eternity   so little known at first.
Is love a turning point?   A reckoning?
I walk the shape my childhood took   under
The sway of pine   the trail unstraight and crooked
By stream and stone   the wet   the green   the
licking
Waters   how could I know this trail is love?

STREET SIGNS FOR A LOVE SONNET:
A LETTER FROM MY IMAGINARY WIFE

Pretty words. A fancy dance you do with phrases,
Mr. Flores, flower man. I pronounce it "Luminous
Bucolic Self Absorption." A remote, a removed un-
rhymed distance in skewered pentameters. Mr. Flores,
my love, you are an anachronism, and struggle
as you will to resurrect a "Troubadour's Pure Heart,"
a "Renaissance Man's Equipoise," the wrestling
will leave you tired, out of step on hard cobblestone
streets decorated with colorful cardboard flags crying:
Mortgage Sale, Mortgage Sale, Mortgage Sale
down these colonial streets, past the monuments
of dead generals riding dead horses. The housing
market has imploded from symbiotic over feeding,
banks have failed from exploded greed, and your
passion without direction will not create compassion,
will not align your heart's compass True North.
Here in the street where trust is a corpse walking
to work every morning, where sunshine is bleached
from most eyes I meet, I rage for equality, then batter
myself for my self-righteous rage. Slowly I've come
to know kind words simply spoken soothe an injured
spirit, heal a damaged heart more than notions
of righting injustices. Perhaps, common courtesy
is civic action enough. Today I lack the faith to lay
down my sword, but pretty words, dancing phrases
turn me in circles I wish to circle. Write.
Love,
Your worse critic

ᏳᎡ
... Letters ...

JADE TREE & PRAYER:
LETTER TO MY IMAGINARY WIFE

Oddly enough, this part of Virginia is a suburb of
Seattle, or so it seems these past weeks of rain, gray
clouds moving through tips of pines on the ridge.
Yesterday, in the sunroom with the placid jade in
the corner, you missed a slightly less than animated
discussion on prayer. The sides were drawn along
these lines: 1.) can make things happen, 2.) can make
the supplicant more peaceful accepting that destiny
will win out and fate will have its way. I think I was
on each side at least once, but was shamed into silence
by the calm demeanor of the jade (she seemed to catch
sunlight just along her many unwagging tongues,
and I am sure she smiled at my often-disquieting
absurdities). After my friends left for Charlottesville
and Maple Drive in Bowling Green, I remembered
with shivers the many times these past 20 years I
prayed for your great smile and laughing ways to come
and tell me that one enormous story we both knew
was pure invention and exaggeration and ultimately
completely untrue. I shiver now because I know I
don't know how to act, or should I say I would not
know how to act day by day with you, especially
when you would demand that I simply be myself. My
argument with God has been centered, essentially, on
the principle that you, humorously of course, would
be a polished mirror to reflect my flaws. Thus, I would
spit-shine this one person enough to abandon any
need for that modern necessity called an ego, and off

we would go (picture us hand in hand) toward those golden roads of heaven. Sometimes in more lucid moments, I think I am a simpleton. Maybe prayer has been less or more effective than I know, but those moments, much like this one, have certainly had their charm.

MARCH & OCCAM'S RAZOR:
A LETTER TO MY IMAGINARY WIFE

At first I thought it was the flu, one of those odd, intense strains that float between acquaintances at the Food Lion, or over coffee at the new Bowling Green café, Jake's Place, on Main Street, but the chills and fever flashes were temporary and not enough to leave me delusional about the weather. Thus, February ended with uncertainty. Morning snow, ice, rain. Afternoon winds, bright sun, then clear sky shifting into heavy draping grey and purple clouds. March seemed steady for a day or two. Cold thrashing winds, oak leaves stampeding like frightened buffalo through the woods down sloping gullies. Nights and immodest, startling stars: the round moon in relief with its tight-lipped thinnest smile. Fields of last year's corn are stubble and browsing deer do not slip into the stand of trees edging the field when I walk near. I mention the weird weather, the peculiar, uncharacteristic behavior of deer, and mysterious happenings among animals (have I written to you of the two-headed albino rat snake on auction on the internet?) as a prelude to an elaborate diatribe on man's nature and its disregard for the courtesies common among frogs. However, I've reduced my original argument to this one phrase: We take more than we give. I desire abundance like the next man, but the abundance I desire is simplification. One Saint said, "I wish you to simplify, simplify, and simplify, to be simple in all aspects of life is to accept life." I think acceptance is like the rocking chair out on my porch where contentment sits and rocks eternal rhythms of joy to lift the folds of leaves rumbling by pretending to be buffalo. Actually, we both know leaves do not pretend to be buffalo, and I pretend only to be what I am. That is what I have to give, that is what I give.

MARCHING FORWARD IN MARCH:
A LETTER FROM MY IMAGINARY WIFE

In this city, morning air is gray, heavy, and often without freshness. Here the country has been confined to a few small parks, anemic trees bracketed in cast iron along cobble stone streets, old fashion gas lamps light at the first hint of twilight, and shops resemble an old world town square. I think the architect of this village had a notion of less complex times, a simple life that seems to ache in the heart of city dwellers like a joyful but forgotten memory .You are not alone in your desires: you may be alone in what you are willing to pay for them. I've read the Saint you quote and question your intent to go the next step: "Be Good, Do Good, Be One." I've come here to do my work, and in that work I am all that I am. Is there a difference between us, if joy is an elusive bubble radiant within us? I walk to work with men and women through gray smog, fog in most eyes I see, but this is the wind to me. It is not enough to discuss life. Didn't the Saint also write, "Truth is high, but higher still is true living"? You have done well to minimize your life, but have you minimized your thinking, have you eliminated the clutching mind? I can't shrink from a challenge, and here in the midst of plenty I have the abundance of emptiness. In truth, it may be easier for me in this ruin than for you in the bucolic glens you haunt among raccoons and squirrels. Glitter catches but does not capture my eye, nor ensnare my heart:

80
... Letters ...

there is too much clatter. The shop windows sell illusions to those needing images. I polish the mirror that keeps no image, no reflection. Write me about the freshness of your day.

ON THE CUSP OF APRIL FOOL'S DAY:
A LETTER FROM MY IMAGINARY WIFE

March is tiresome, tedious rumors of rain and snow,
a heavy sky low and laboring most days. Gray
mornings I walk less briskly battered sideways
along cobble stone streets, the new blossoms on the
Bradford pear trees are frozen, stiff in harsh winds,
especially northern winds. It may be the cold, but
sometimes I think my fellow pedestrians lug sorrow
like a sack of worms and it takes the rhythm out of
their step. The question that gnaws at me is, "Are
they walking toward something loved, or away from
something feared"? I don't believe in "Seasonal
Disorders," but I believe in your disorder. My theory
is winter is less entertaining, less enthralling, and the
psychic misery comes to the front of the stage, but
is wordless from years of being ignored. It aches,
silently, and that playful spirit we were born with
recedes beyond grasp. Part II. of my theory is, in the
summer we escape in nature's amusement park. There
is a koan that asks: "Where do you go to hide from
yourself"? I believe it is a season, not a place. What
is that prayer you always repeat, "Lord grant me the
courage to change the things that I can, the serenity
to accept the things that I can't, and the wisdom to
know the difference"? I try to remember this prayer
walking these March streets. Do you think it uplifts
this dreary atmosphere? This city is not the ambience
of your monastic retreat in the woods. How are the
wooded paths down by the swamp, home to skunk

and raccoon? Are beavers building again, or has this drought left them speechless, squatting on crackling banks? Are squirrels mad in passion now: so small, so noisy, so enthusiastic. Here "a fast nickel beats a slow dime." It is not the same passion, not the same enthusiasm. I imagine you are beginning to bubble, celebrating April Fool's Day with yourself imposed silence. Perhaps you know more than you are telling me: more, perhaps, than I would believe. What do you think of my theory, my love?

APRIL FIRST CONFESSIONS OF A FOOL: A LETTER TO MY IMAGINARY WIFE

April has never been a cruel month for me, spring winds lifting branches and new buds, daffodils a radiant yellow, grass greener than an Irishman's imagination. So much happens here, it is hard to cull the most exotic, but one slow, overweight ground hog lumber- loped across a field of corn stubbles, and slid under the forsythia by the edge of the road, the forsythia with spiking yellow tendrils, the same forsythia the cottontail hunched in shadow to become invisible, ears flat back an instant before it leapt straight to those mean blackberry thickets. Blackberry thickets are not mean, I hear your voice say in the back of my head, but they do bite finger and shin nonetheless. Do you remember who wrote: "Again in the country, I have come to realize / I am no longer envious / of the common quality of grass"? I don't know what this means, but imagine it speaks to some esoteric quality of love. Love has made me a fool a time or two, but fortunately time is infinite, forgiving, and forgetful. All through sad-gray March I practiced my smile, summer will be sweltering, sticky, embracing and I need to be prepared for the upsurge of undiluted green, honeysuckle yellow and delightful flickering in the wind in the woods. Do you think it is a simpleton's sexual exaggeration to say, "I'm a bud about to burst"?

APRIL AMENDS:
A LETTER FROM MY IMAGINARY WIFE

Flores, flower-power, Mackie, I'm being silly,
coquettish, making amends for my blustering,
boisterous, bludgeoning onomatopoeia diatribes. A
chemical imbalance, in the wrong phrase of the moon
for writing, mea culpa. I was in the Red Tent. The
curse of Eve. Childless, I make "the ills of the earth"
my offspring, and the tireless and endless efforts to
correct my children have me frustrated past endurance.
Motherhood, it clings to my bones, and no matter how
deep into the earth I put my hands, or how high in the
heavens my head, my heart aches in a hollow place
for this absence. I think you have always considered
ideas your children, and dress them in their Sunday
best to navigate the wobbly world spindle-legged, but
on their own. You have a detached, aesthetic distance
from your progeny I lack. Does feeling insecure,
incomplete in myself cause me discomfort, and to
imagine flaws in everything and everybody around
me? Hypocrisy is ramped. I support the women
marching around abortion clinics. But why do they
march halfway? Why do they not equally march
around penitentiaries executing the living? Isn't life
sacred from conception to the grave? This is a good
end stop: I'm gaining my equilibrium, and prefer
equipoise to ranker at the moment. Excuse me my
peccadilloes, large and armored as armadillos, as I will
extend to you the same grace.

ೞ
... Letters ...

CHECKING ACCOUNT:
A LETTER TO MY IMAGINARY WIFE

It defies the imagination and logic why I cannot balance my checking account. I blame it on spring, but all winter I calculated the same numbers: wrong numbers. Dogwoods have flowered like ponds of white floating, drifting away on the wind. Oak, maple, hickory have spread a green layer of pollen on everything. Peach, pear, plum, cherry trees have brilliant green leaves, and look like they just had a surprising idea and are excited about it. This morning the only sounds I heard were the buzz of carpenter bees, and one bird's absolutely pure love song piercing the woods. Heavy clouds shift up from the south. It seems I notice flowering trees, birds in love, bees at work with more accuracy than the numbers in my checking account. Was it Hafez dropped a pebble in an earthen jug for his every wrong, and was shocked to see so many pebbles at the end of the day? Counting pebbles is alchemy. Common stones transformed into diamonds, and diamonds cut to the purity of perception. Does it matter that I can't account for bus fare? Now it's raining. A good rain rattling everything. Distant, faint thunder, no lightning. I think change is not the sound of rumbling thunder, but is the sound of one pebble hitting an earthen jug.

NIGHT RAIN & CANDLELIGHT & SILENCE & SHADOWS: A LETTER TO MY IMAGINARY WIFE

Lightning flashes in the trees, thunder, then a lull palpable as a hand on the shoulder. The smell of rain has been in the air all day. Now the night rain bends branches where this morning a brown owl swooped in a graceful arc inches above the underbrush and vanished in a blur of green leaves. Rain tattoos intricate designs on the roof as winds push it south. How lovely and romantic it would be to write that this candlelight has some mystical connection with the rhythm of the rain ---stretching out its slender neck like some turtle from its shell when the speed of the wind picks up and rain glides by leaving a sort of silence, for a moment, in its wake---but I cannot write that. Both rain and candlelight seem to move to their own nature. You have asked why this 18th. century life in the woods? Why not DC, Baltimore, or New York, or some city--- any city--- with excitement, with people breathing hard right there on the edge? At this moment, I know less is more, and that in the small silences the wind makes in the rain, I can hear my heart most distinctly, most clearly. You are perfectly right in pointing out that desire has nothing to do with people, places, and things---and everything to do with the composition of the heart. When I get up from this table, walk across this room to stare out the window at the storm, (although I can see nothing but silver trees in lightning flashes), my movements disturb the candlelight. Distorted shadows creep along these log walls. Sitting back at the table, I write with pen and shadow of the pen. I think this is like the spirit's partnership in everything. More often than not, I don't see this except in those special angles of light. With all the distorted movement in most cities, wouldn't it be difficult to get the right angle of light? Perhaps if I had greater confidence in my heart's understanding, I would not have to ask this question of you.

A LETTER TO MY IMAGINARY WIFE FROM THE AMUSEMENT PARK

Isabel blew out the lights, bent trees to resemble fat men attempting to touch their toes. Days before branches snapped the power lines, farmers turned high corn to stubble, and on every other foot of the road, a silk-worm or fuzzy brown caterpillar humped, scooted toward the woods. Sky was scrubbed clear blue, air without summer's damp heat. Now it is 9:00 p.m. and this cabin is incredibly dark outside the sphere of these two candles. When I watched Isabel work through the trees, I had the sense of an enormous vacuum cleaner --- the stand-up type with rows of whirling brushes ---sucking up dirt and debris embedded in the fibers of God's good rug --- perhaps cleaning for weekend guests? There is something to the notion of impermanence. Are we, at best, season ticket holders in this amusement park, with not much more significance than our idea of ourselves to sustain us? If we know the ride's start and finish gate are the same, is the trick to learn to go jolly on the ride? You are a woman intimate with the seasons, reply quickly.

CR
... *Letters* ...

APRIL WAVES SETTLE:
A LETTER FROM MY IMAGINARY WIFE

Recently, Dear James, in high dudgeon I wrote you
of the molten metal whirling around my heart, my
head. Now a sort of post orgasmic tranquility has
tenuously settled me into my bones, but I will not be
encased in inaction. This morning in pristine light I
stood looking at a cherry tree in bloom, an expansive
pink cloud wobbling in the wind, and this peace was
invaded by ripped up trees, tossed-over trailer homes,
twisted lives, shattered boards the tornadoes left
crashing through the Midwest this week. These images
were bad, but worse to hear that slick, pimp of Biblical
purity, Jack Van Impe tell his TV audience every
tragedy marks the coming rapture, and God's judgment
on sinful America. His pronouncement was the
cruelest destruction. He did not mention governmental
complicity with pharmaceutical companies to leave on
the market ingredients to make methamphetamines.
This drug is the epidemic eating hearts and making
the homeless. Profit + ruined = the zero sum. Do
you think me a dunderhead for walking away from
the idyllic charms you wonder in hopes of bumping
into enlightenment? Isn't there some Buddhist
notion about staying in the cycle of incarnations until
everybody has achieved enlightened? Isn't feeling
a hacksaw sawing my rib cage because of my own
comforts the same notion? Why do others go without
1.) a place to live, 2.) running water I can drink

without disease, 3.) electricity, 4.) food in the icebox. My luxuries one and all. My malaise leaves me sleepless. My mottled gushing is bred of frustration; less today, as I retreat behind words, a labyrinth of language designed to obfuscate. I would reach out to you, but my fingers are cold.

MOBIUS STRIP:
A LETTER TO MY IMAGINARY WIFE

Rain rolled over the hill out of a dark stillness. Have
I told you my definition of time? Azaleas bloom red,
carpenter bees drill the porch beams, weeds wobble
to my knees, swallows make a nest above the front
door. Moss tuffs, mud flakes, twigs on the welcome
mat, cold nights, clear stars, windy mornings, bright
sun. Azalea blooms drop off, carpenter bees disappear
behind their papier-mâché' doors, and maples, oaks,
hickories are waves of green. My world shrinks and
expands in undulating moments defining nothing. I
can't remember the last time I spoke to another person,
but it was colder, darker earlier. Perhaps months
alone crystallized my thinking, created a shorthand
that does not translate well, and just when I realize
God could not create a worse hell than listening to my
septic thinking, the script flips, and angels sing. I can't
square a circle, but I've learned to purr like a cat.

AT THE EDGE OF DARKENING WOODS:
A SONNET FOR MY IMAGINARY WIFE

Winter has gone in snow and wind. A hard
Freeze caught the buds in bloom and white on pear
And apple trees near fields I walk with heart
Raging to slip the body's knot   to tear
My rooted spirit from its rooted bones.
The clouds are arched above the pines   daisies
Bob and weave in the wind that sweeps along
The wintered grass. My life steps by one day
By one day in agony and stillness.
The dark seeps to the edge of woods   the air,
This country air   is crisp   an April chill.
Can lung and throat now scream the spirit bare?
I walk the fields to darkened woods and know
The path is narrow   night   unrelentingly slow.

ONCE UPON A TIME
BLACKBERRIES IN A PAIL:
A SONNET FOR MY IMAGINARY WIFE

The grass is mowed   the flower beds are plucked
Of weeds   the trellis dug in   set   and braced
For lilacs   rose   and bushy honeysuckle.
The fields are green   June green   but still a trace
Of winter lingers on in ragged brown
Oak leaves that curl beneath the scrub windrows.
The blackberries soon will be red and round
On spiked   thin stems that darken rich   and glow
Almost a luminous   it seemed   deep green.
When I was young and berry picking   pail
In hand   and new to woods   my brother teamed
Me with a sister and   we lost the trail
The others marked   but now I laugh and pass
The thickets lost in things that do not last.

APRIL SPRINGS AND ENOUGH IS ENOUGH:
A LETTER FROM MY IMAGINARY WIFE

James, Dear James, "I think, therefore I am" is the handle on the spade I'm using to dig my garden. The afterlife, reincarnation, karma doesn't cut it for me. I've cracked open enough fortune cookies to know fortune is what I make of it. Astrology, tarot cards, tea leaves, I-Ch'ing, psychic hotlines are not going to save the rain forests, restore rivers and bays, halt melting polar caps, stop rock throwing in the Middle East, end the Janjaweed's rape and murder of every living thing in Darfur, or bring back any of the extinct species bulldozed over on the way to the paradise of progress. You can walk all the backwoods trails and talk to birds and squirrel like your hero St. Francis, but that is not getting illegals in your county one day closer to safety. I walk dusty April streets, March the driest on record, and the brush along the roads is waiting to explode. I'm exploding. I've had enough. I'm going to get my sign, red, white and blue lettering, "FREEDOM TO WORK," and will take the bus to support those high school kids walking out of their schools to protect their parents from deportation. Has anybody asked the Sioux, Apache, Navaho, Comanche what they think of illegal immigrants? Do you remember the big political noise in Washington about South African Apartheid? What is a reservation? Does the hypocrisy make you crazy? I hear your melodious monk's voice tell me, "It's spring madness, it's your "élan vital," your woman spirit, causing turmoil between your five elements: your wild chi clanging metal, banging wood, boiling water, stoking fire, pounding earth, and making me a muddled mass about to give birth to a Universe." No, Mackie, No. My heart aches. My head aches. I think, and therefore I act. I'll keep you in the loop.

THE FIRST DAY OF SPRING:
A LETTER FROM MY IMAGINARY WIFE

I woke to a parallel universe this first day of Spring.
Snowstorms bury Nebraska, Colorado shudders in the
white stuff, and all the Bradford pear trees exploding
into enormous white clouds making quaint country
lanes of these drab streets. You write raccoons,
possums raid your porch, I have roving gangs of
teenage thugs randomly beating, robbing unsuspecting
window shoppers. This first day of Spring is the 3rd
anniversary of the war in Iraq. Can we expect other
than the brutal from our young? I imagine you have
been dribbling on about the equinox, yin and yang,
chiaroscuro, alignment of planets and celestial bliss
like some lambent patina bubbling in your spirit.
All from the nebulous, tenuous moment when light
appears to balance on a blade of grass? How easy
it is to be obsessed with a notion. I've moved past
argument, momentum stirs my blood in a primal and
visceral swelling ---Spring--- Spring even in this cold
speaks to me. I'm comfortable with snowflakes and
pear blossoms equally. I have no earth to put my
hands in, but I will put my head in the sky, my heart
in the wind, and embrace my work at the end of this
dingy street with the love
Spring earth cradles its first wobbling blades of grass.

CR
... £etters ...

A LITTLE SUMMER RAIN,
A LITTLE MIRICLE:
A SONNET FOR MY IMAGINARY WIFE

Are things on which the dazzled senses rest
JK

Are things on which the dazzled senses rest
The things I can deny myself and be
The man I would become? Is it a test?
Pressure builds to breaking, and sweet release

Is green, a rain so soft it flicks the leaves,
And barely bends a blade of grass. The wind,
A tickle more or less, its strength to heave
The branches here and there has gone, has been

The bane two days before this quiet rain
Began its low, its throaty hum I hear.
A joy, almost a lightness lighting frame
By frame my fractured heart congealed by fear

These years, denied no more. I can adore
Spicy bursts of green and much, so much more.

DRAFT # 7 OF 11 FRAGMENTED MEMORIES: NOTES FOR A LETTER TO MY IMAGINARY WIFE

Rocks sparkled   flecks of light
                  red earth
     a dog's bark evaporated gray
in the gray air   maybe   June
the first of June   was it here I left
wet footsteps on slab rock
I knew my days in a spin   and kissed
       years first born of the sun

          my age was water

and sought no reason to explain youth
was young   fragile   often numb
to the edge it cut
    this is pine
this is elm   this is cottonwood   green
folded leaves and green sloped branches
        slipped into shadows
heavy gray in the east
hung above mountains
       streaks of lightning
         in the air
      rain on the low hills
      I stepped in and out
of my breath
leading me into shifting winds

            CR
     ... *Letters* ...

into voices wailing

what miracles played out

in my eyes

a clear path

cut to the horizon   through shadows

woven above water and rock

A LOVE SONNET:
FOR MY IMAGINARY WIFE

From fairest creature we desire increase
                                    W.S.

Sunshine   the sun   so easy saying this
But rain   the rain was day and night and day
It seemed untethered thoughts would float and
spin
My head in self-sustaining light   away

In light for love   for you I think   as down
This slope   this trail under young pines all green
Against a cloudless sky   no wind   or sound
On this soft bedded slope   the ground and leaves

Completely soaked   and like my heart   is filled
With brimming strength enough to stand me straight
And take my breath away   I stand   am still
And after just a moment feel as great

The day was meant to be   and light increase
From fairest creature   we desire   increase.

CR
... Letters ...

GOBBLEDEGOOK FOR A LOVE SONNET:
A LETTER FROM MY IMAGINARY WIFE

Gobbledegook, what more, my flower man, to describe
"A Love Sonnet," the words all pretty and posed,
rhyme and meter, more or less, on the mark, and what
"X," and where the "X" is the mark? "Self-sustaining
light"? Perhaps no more accurate statement needs
making by me. Days ago at the dumpster large and
green in the alley, stuck wadded in weeds and bushes,
paper lost from evicted neighbors cluttered and blew
about in ugliness and litter. Duty bound, I picked up
the trash, and among this wayfaring homeless tribe
of papers found this page I send to you --- author &
publication both lost to frayed paper --- and explains
my gobbledegook pronouncement
on "A Love Sonnet":
                    HOMELESS

                              for Governor George Allen

When northern winds settled this august,
southern city, pigeons froze to telephone wires,
and the homes of homeless men, men that worked

roads, worked odd day jobs, and lived
nights under Dock Street Bridge ---
was bulldozed. The one oil-drum furnace black

from long fires, and stacked firewood, pitched
cardboard shelters, boxes of food, boxes of clothes,
creased photographs of gone families, gone

girlfriends all bulldozed into the dropping
temperature. On the street the men talk about
the new governor sworn in the Saturday before

the Friday bulldozers of this old southern city
pushed their oil-drum, pushed their fire wood,
pushed their clothes, pushed their photographs,

pushed the heart of their home into one
enormous mound stilled by freezing winds.
The men speak to their vacant street,

speak to themselves under their bridge,
speak about the home burning in their heart,
and how there are many, many, who are homeless.

My lost rower, my flower man, my dear Mr. Flores,
keep stroking the wide waters of your sea, and send
in a bottle, a bluebottle, your seashells to ring in my
still untamed, untuned ears here in a city of hard
cobblestone streets, monuments to the dead, and wads
of ugly papers afloat.

ᑭ
... *Letters* ...

INNER SPANIARD:
A LETTER FROM MY IMAGINARY WIFE

Normally, I begin with the most egregious events:
poached elephants and the increased ivory trade in the
Congo, or recent rumors floating around Washington
of a plan to change diplomacy into invasion of Iran
and the utility of bunker busting bombs, but I imagine
you are not aware of these events or of millions of
Hispanics on the march. Mackie, Flores, your kinsmen
are in the streets demanding their rights and protection
by law, demanding Democracy in the America they
have made home. Now is the time to make right what
your father made wrong: reclaim your heritage, get in
touch with your inner Spaniard, Mr. Flores. Your father
was a first-born Spanish American, your grandparents
sailed here young, excited, leaving aristocratic lives
on the continent. Is that ancestry something to deny?
Why deepen your father's misguided footsteps toward
the British Isles? Is a pure bloodline essential for
anything other than breeding dogs, horses, cows?
How does karma, an elemental part of your cosmology,
fit "selective breeding"? Didn't all the Saints and
mystics decry the caste system? I realize you may
not be concerned, bobbing around bucolic pastures,
idyllic trails through wooded hills, but larger ills
abound: 1.) Kashmir a shambles with little food and
few shelters, 2.) CEO's robbing company stores and
taking pensioner's retirement, 3.) politicians peddling
dishonesty, 4.) and rise in drug induced crime. I'm

leaving to join the marchers, white t-shirt sparkling white, and would have you walk with me. Can't you change one heart at a time when many hearts are joined together?

RAVANIOUS BEES DELIGHT:
A LETTER TO MY IMAGINARY WIFE

Feral cats screeching in heat, escaped hunting beagles
catching the scent nosing around leaves, white tailed
deer dodging down trees in a panic, and even the
myoptic possum under the azaleas make less racket
than graceful carpenter bees swooping, looping,
floating in stillness the envy of any hummingbird, as
they reduce this shack to rubble. Board thin walls hum
to their gnawing after swooning meals in blood-red
azaleas, and this swarm chewing wood by sunlight and
moonlight confirms the cliché, "busy as a bee." Will
sawdust walls hold the roof, this monastery for one run
down to bluebells, bluebells spattering green mounds
along the path, bluebells sprinkled about this shack
surrounded by uprooted pines leaning on maples, oaks,
hickory. Winter and winds were savage this past year,
spring rains and winds tossed shallow rooted pines like
scattered pick-up sticks. Now, from the remains of the
droning shack, I send:

HERE THERE THERE HERE

Grass blades sparkle   morning rain
Small wind   another   small wind

Gray sky   distant train   hollow
Low long note   a moment   holds
Completely   all emptiness

my new poem for your pleasure in your leisure
in the city.

ℯ

... Letters ...

SILK ROAD:
A LETTER TO MY IMAGINARY WIFE

Did a season of migration down a remembered route awakened them? Those are not round river stones suddenly sprung legs and learned to walk. Turtle or tortoise? Box Turtle. I stay with names learned in childhood woods stumbling tree roots, jutting rocks, water from nowhere puddled mysteriously under spreading ferns, dodging that strange plant smelling like skunk. We called them Box turtles, that strange green was Skunk Cabbage. A caravan of Box Turtles passed over the gravel island of rock and back into woods dark, their road rain soaked oak leaves, and light filtered through high pines dappling the ground. They must know they are invisible, but not invincible balanced on all fours, looking, breathlessly still it seems, blended in color and light. I practice that stillness, the artless motionless motion, without the aid of a Halloween orange good as any dappled sunlight on brown earth. Here then not here, almost a trick of vision or velocity or neither, it is that magical. How to be completely transparent, present to all my surrounds, the invisible visible? A mirror, I think I will become a mirror, and for you my love, hand held and artlessly visible. Write from your city.

FIELDS OF CORN:
A LETTER TO MY IMAGINARY WIFE

The August corn is a foot over my head, but that is
not to say it is particularly tall as I am not big on the
outside. When I walk narrow country roads past fields
of corn in first morning light, I sometimes imagine
the clouds of fog above the deep green stalks are
sucked down through the corn's tasseled heads, and
these clouds explode, and swell each wrapped ear of
corn wobbling in a country wind. Some may think
it is a pure homespun fantasy that I believe if I walk
past any field of corn with peace in my heart it will be
absorbed --- through some strange form of osmosis
--- and eventually pop out, like so much popcorn, as
thoughtful gestures, or comforting words somewhere
in the world. But in a flimsy attempt to be less
mystical, I walk these country roads with a plastic bag,
and pick out of thorny bushes McDonalds wrappers,
Pepsi cans, Budweiser and Michelob bottles. I rattle
making this part of Caroline County cleaner one
wrapper, one can, one bottle at a time. The enormous
bald eagle perched on the old, bleached-white pine
branch jutting out over young pines was exceptional in
all his white-feathered charisma and hunting flight, but
I am equally designed and built to find my prey dirt-
covered and dull under the bushes.

80
... £etters ...

100 % ALL NATURAL INGREDIANTS:
A LETTER FROM MY IMAGINARY WIFE

It's an insult to my sex. Victoria's Secret, glossy
women windswept and wet on white sand beaches,
contours the making of the "miracle bra" posed by
contortionists. Is this the "miracle" of contortions or
distortions? Who is fooled by this? Who is deluded
into believing this is something natural, something to
emulate, to strive to be or achieve? No wonder there
are many women sticking their fingers down their
throats, or starving themselves for an unreal image.
And to achieve what end? Love? Sex? It cannot be
love, and there is not enough health for sex. Isn't sex
the thing you have now given up for God? I know
your running joke about how you spend hours naming
each little fellow as you glue on its tail, then those
swimming lessons, and how difficult it is for them to
wear floatation devises until they learn to swim on
their own, and how you encourage them to "swim for
your lives boys." After such nurturing, are you afraid
they will drown in choppy waters? Is that why you
have given up what other men take medicine to do?
There is nothing artificial in love or its arts. We were
100 % all natural ingredients those timeless times we
shared the evening stars. I'm leaving for work. I walk
by a cherry tree blooming pink-red in morning light.
This tree's fullness fills me up.

RAGE & RAGE & RAGE:
READING THE NEWSPAPER
IN THE CITY OF COBBLE STONE STREETS:
A LETTER FROM MY IMAGINARY WIFE

FLOGGED A WOMAN IN
PAKISTAN. Thirty strokes.
Thirty strokes cheered by
bearded men & in the center
one woman. Thirty strokes.
One woman circled by men,
heads wrapped in black cloth,
righteous cloth, cloth of some
spoken or touted Koranic law,
cloth of oppression. It's the
21st Century: PUBLIC FLOG-
GING? & this will appease
God, & this will bring PUR-
ITY to that dog-kicking country
of knee-bending, bowing men?
Facing east a necessity? What-
ever direction they face, is the
wrong direction: it's wrong-
headed when their hearts are
dry pumps, when their mouths
only know the taste of sand.
I was epileptic, I twitched
in waves of rage, rage like
that Italian earthquake's
epicenter was my naval. Con-

fused, ultimately I didn't know
which direction to turn, my
heart broken by the earth re-
settling itself in Italy, & the
natural flow of innocent
turmoil visited on an ancient
land, & my heart swelled to
reach any bloody, buried hand,
& in rage I knew only con-
fusion, confused to understand
how, how do men impose
cruelty on others when living
on an earth creating pain &
destruction in its innocent
turnings? Exhausted, rage is
exhausting. I'm late to work,
tired in tired shoes I've not
put on the cobblestone streets,
but Dogwoods, Bradford pears,
Chinese cherry trees are
blooming in the light morning
wind, miniature clods hovering
above the street walks, & I
know every tired step will be
less burdensome, lighter step
by step. Blossoms & blooms,
my heart opens. Charm me,
enchant me with your music,
send your sonnets.

CR
... *Letters* ...

SHADOW CAVE:
A SONNET FOR MY IMAGINARY WIFE

The silver clouds, far – far away to leave
JK

The silver clouds, far – far away to leave
So little sparkling rain on peach and pear

with bees   buzzing the country air   no tree
Seems motionless against the blue   now bare

And open sky.   I stand   a silent man
Alone in pines   in shade the sun has made

Into a tranquil shadow cave.   I stand
And listen   bees too far to hear   this cave

Of shadows down the hill and edged against
The deeper forest dark and dense   too far

Too far away to hear the drone   intense
It is   I know   this dance from branch and star

White-flowers blooming branch on branch. In shade
I rest   no clouds   no rain   no bees   to evade.

UNDER A TREE LOOKING FOR THE FOREST:
A SONNET FOR MY IMAGINARY WIFE

They also serve who only stand and wait.
JM

They also serve to hold the soil in place,
These maples, oaks, and sycamores that skirt
The grassy edge we walk to follow traces
The deer in startled leaps have left in dirt,

And leaves now scattered near the bushes, rocks
So hard to get around or past. This trail
Is known to them, it seems, but we are blocked,
Not able leapers, not as startled. Sail

We would if capable. Alas, we are
Unwinged for now, and all intentions, good
Or bad amount to air unmoved, and bear
A sort of sad and tired witness should

We care to count the many fingers fate
Has held up for who only stand and wait.

MEMO

TO: A Troubadour

FROM: Imaginary Wife

SUBJECT: Wrong Century

Sonnet? Oh, to be a golden haired Princess
sequestered high in the highest castle tower [bower?]
for only there will I find the true import of your poems
to be otherwise not from this century.

THIRTEEN PENNIES & WHAT HAVE YOU GOT:
A SONNET FOR MY IMAGINARY WIFE

It's odd to find a penny but thirteen?
No joke, right by my foot I saw just one
Then scattered all about, a few between
The pebbles near some grass and rocks, and some
Almost a loss to lack of paying not
A bit of mind to what I do, or see.
Always amazes me just how a dot
Of blindness grows until, at times, for me,
I live the clarity of mud, but think
Unknowns, unseen are things to tease a few;
Not me a bit, however, taken in
By such a muck, by such a wanton spew.
A penny whistle, penny for a thought,
I've found thirteen, and what have I been taught?

HIGH DESERT REAL ESTATE:
A LETTER TO MY IMAGINARY WIFE
FROM SCOTTSDALE, ARIZONA

May is the month of dismay.
      Early and late in the falling
tumble of days, my most precious loves slipped away
in less movement than the flutter of a butterfly's wing,
in less time than a raindrop falling. Now in the middle
of the beginning and end, I stand under one expanse of
aquatic blue sky [better color for ocean than air] end-
to-end of this high desert. It is hot. Wind is no friend.
Dry wind, winds in gusts sweep dust along dusty
trials. Time is a forgotten idea on the high desert. One
moment, one moment, and abacus beads shift, add the
sum of days until no bead moves more.
      Barrel cactus
fringed in tulip shaped red flower pods [red deeper red
than any red rose] saguaro cactus flower white on its
fingertips, not an inch not glistening in white quill-
needles, and birds land beside flowers on their pudgy
fingers without a "by your leave" or hesitant motion.
Texas Yellow Stars flower puff into low
yellow clouds shooting along the sand, oleander in
a high hedgerow blasting white flowers clusters into
every passing, rasping dry wind, declare this high
desert in bloom spot on the middle of my agony.
     Once covered wagons
battered by dusty grit creaked over gully, gulch and
wash, cursed every unsettled day to greener lands to

settle. Range Rovers now creep rough trails between sage, tumbleweeds, ocotillos, stately
and occasional saguaro, exploring land selling in "6 figures an acre."

Empty hands begin, empty hands end
the passing over this dusty ground, this real estate investment. One moment, one shifting bead is between now and the flutter of a butterfly's wing. Over my cherished real state, over my heart tuned to the smallest dry wind passing, I hold my open hand.

CODA: HIGH DESERT REAL ESTATE: A LETTER TO MY IMAGINARY WIFE FROM SCOTTSDALE, ARIZONA

Round moon in the middle,
a light night sky, mountains black shapes on distant
ridges. Distorted in moonlight shrub, low tree,
cactus become indistinguishable, amorphous shapes,
scattered, dense ghosts or corporal phantoms dark
against night's darkness. Night chills. Windless. One
star east, one west and their longing is palpable.
                              Tarantula, scorpion,
centipede, snake, artful field mouse, dodging
jackrabbit all out-and-about dusty lanes in this place
they know as home. Crickets in harmony have not
ended the first movement of their symphony.
Stillness embraces the least sound. A hollow-throated
Harley Davidson pattering down a far road is long
fading.
                                            Held
in this lessening moonlight, I listen to my heart's
reaching, my heart's grasping what is less than a wisp
of dry wind not bending a stalk of prairie grass, listen
to my heart turn to a choir settling in to strike up a
music composed by ancient masters, music fainter than
a butterfly's heartbeat, and my heart in its listening
way will open as the tempo mounts, the intensity
builds to shake bone, boulder, leaf, and flower into
an ecstasy of tears and love for nothing gone for all
eternity.

POSTSCRIPT TO HIGH DESERT REAL ESTATE & CODA:
A LETTER TO MY IMAGINARY WIFE

Nightly the pale dark darkens. Less moon, more stars.
Vision moves inward, light moves outward.

Tranquility and equipoise through damp grasses giving
rhythm to each step.

Walking becomes dance, breathing song. All harmony
envelopes the spheres harmony, nothing is unattended.

Can love be described otherwise?

PEACE IN THE VALLEY:
NOTES FOR A POEM TO MY IMAGINARY
WIFE: SCOTTSDALE, ARIZONA

Unthrottled sun   heat ripples in the distance
sand and wind   wind and sand   I cried

a month and the absence of sadness is not joy
spirit in the blood   spirit in the bones   earth

to air   air to earth   in the middle   bougainvillea
blooming rosy red and delightful   oleanders white

clouds close to the earth   the sky empty
empty beyond the thought of clouds   one dove

on top of a saguaro   cluster of white flowers circling
its legs   one plaintive call   another   turns
calls   turns   head tilts   angles and looks   calls
circles   almost a complete circle   head tilts

waits   flies east down into mesquite wood shrubs
and yellow flowers do not ripple   do not move

late afternoon   trees bend   high tips dipping
in a slight wind   shadows longer   heat at its

peak   and now it seems nothing moves   dust
releases spirit   just a gentle shift   nothing moves
and   everything blooms   flowering in delight
this is the way   this is peace in the valley.

∞
... £etters ...

JUNE BRIDE: A SLENDER VOLUME OF POETRY FOUND IN THE WOODS: A LETTER TO MY IMAGINARY WIFE

What do you make of this, the first and last poems
in JUNE BRIDE, a slender volume of poems left
on the flat rock above the swamp, the rock named,
"Philosopher's Throne" for the notions hatched sitting
there watching cattails and reeds catching winds above
brackish water.

IN THE KINGDOM OF LEAVES

A one room country church
Frosted windows and white gowns

Side by side
Together in the name of God

Not to be lead into Temptation
This gold the heart's symbol exchanged

Solemn words, quick glances
Circles and circle of promise

Bound into the floating colors of leaves
Hearts humming the one hymn of morning

Hands hold, arms embrace, one breath in light
In the Kingdom of Leaves.

ଓଃ
... *Letters* ...

THE END OF LOVE

One window is rain streaked.
Red lipstick on white, crushed cigarette butts.
His hysterical voice, a violent pitch.
Many children thickened her body.
Trees in a row hide overgrown weeds, the house.
No picture hangs straight on the walls.
A large reproduction of an eternally still landscape
Tilts broken in its frame.
She leaned on the door, unsteady.
He walked through the room, walked down the road.

Rain came up suddenly, some squall from over the
low rise got up, and coming down in fists and fingers
jabbing, just made the cabin completely wet, the book
dry, unsmudged. After reading JUNE BRIDE, the
fire down to its last skimpy log, and stars absolutely
blasting the night, my love, to you in the city I send
my first poem of troubling love, and wait your missive
from city streets cobble stoned and cold.

UNTITLED

A noisy shadow bangs the trees
Above my head
My heart ferments
This hackneyed rhyme   in time   for thee.

A MONTH OF SUMMER RAIN:
A LETTER OF REBUTTAL
TO MY IMAGINARY WIFE

Pines and oaks, the tall ones on the ridge, were half in
fog, and corn was solid green to the hill deer vanish at
night after they have eaten the most tender shoots of
my plum and peach trees. I describe the weather, the
shape wind takes through trees and fields, the rows of
earth I plow, the patch of grass and weeds I cut that
you may know my otherworldly tendencies are, at
times, earth bound. The discussion, and corresponding
implications, on planet alignment and movement,
as they affect the cosmic order and beginning of the
Golden Age could be conceived as gossamer. Practical
application of divine laws has remained difficult for
me. Perhaps there is some merit in your description of
my behavior as "absent and ethereal." Good intentions,
which have paved many of my roads, are not lacking,
but design and direction need greater consideration.
To this end, I implore you to offer suggestions. I
know you have mastered the art of baking bread,
preparing a meal almost wholly out of thin air which
you serve with the lightest flavorings of humorous
and instructive stories that leave me breathless, but I
require something more particular, more concrete. Is
it proper to describe my needs as "cave paintings"?
The day has grown long in the tooth, and I, although
missing your instructions, have rocks to haul out of the
field to the wall holding the hill's erosion back.

附
... £etters ...

TWO DAYS BEFORE THE EQUINOX:
A LETTER TO MY IMAGINARY WIFE

It is a couple of hours past noon, bright sun, this
morning's throttling winds have taken a rest, shadows
on the road are braced in stillness, and I find myself
moving toward balance, and internal equipoise equal
to the balance of day and night. I once read in a
poem: "Time was when time wasn't / more than the
movement of the yellow sun." A slight wobble in low
bushes, a ground swell beginning, and perhaps the
wind may build again, but the sky is pure blue, pure
light. Does the Tao say "divide by one and you have
the ten thousand things"? I believe time is elastic,
and my proof: a joyful moment is quicker than a sad
moment. Have you ever wondered why squirrels are
gray? One of the little rascals just hopped across
the road and sits on the granite rock embankment.
He blends, almost disappears, a natural enough
occurrence, but the oaks, pine, maples are not near that
color this time of the year. What to make of that? You
think me "flighty," suggest medications, a modern aide
for an outdated troubadour's wondering inspirations,
with no dulcet strains describing it, is offhandedly
referred to as "suffering the varieties of ADD," or that
other "de jour diagnosis," Bipolar Disorder NOS that
thralls doctors and HMO's equally. Will you entertain
an alternate name for my malaise? Would you
consider naming it "A moment?" Would you consider
a moment, this moment, the moment, scintillating in
its own luxury blending seamlessly, not more magical

than squirrel and rock, a less cumbersome diagnosis to describe me? My love suffers from "a moment," the doctors are not clear how to proceed. I offer you moments of charming conversation, as I find this moment charm enough for me.

NOTES FOR A LETTER
TO MY IMAGINARY WIFE

Two days the gray sky teased,
with a light mist, white flowers
on the dogwood trees.

Unsolicited memories, a turmoil
in many tongues, argued
the nature of love, the utility of anger.

I carried worms of indignation,
a burlap bag full, up hills, and
white flowers moaned in the mist,

although this more exaggeration
than memory or actual fact.
But this image prevails:

traces of translucent Queen Anne's Lace
and bees crowned in gold
above April vines draping the fence are factual.

Again gray mist neither earth
nor sky tosses about glimpses
of this person, that place, this time.

Childhood found, childhood lost?
Rhythms of speech trudge over hills
in mist containing no shapes, no facts.

ଌ
... Letters ...

LONG ISLAND EXPRESS:
A TRAVEL LETTER TO MY IMAGINARY WIFE

the crooked roads are the roads of genius
James Stephens

Day Before Day One

Packed my father's leather satchel, its better days in
Europe gone. Sky gray the whole day, unannounced
threats in dense stillness indicate rain. Green seems
richer in texture, more complete, trees full in their
stride. Green on green, white dogwoods speckled here
and there pronounce the depth, intensifies the quiet,
even gray squirrels leap less high and slower in this
translucent molasses, this last of the day.

Nothing fancy --- jeans, blue work shirts, strong foot
wear, thick socks --- comfort for the long haul leaving
the owl to hoot morning light over the eastern ridge,
carpenter bees to disassemble this shack at their
leisure, hummingbird in love
to hover and swoon into azaleas alone in passion, and
gray rock entertain the rain.

I go after all emptiness, go where the long, low note
evaporates in the 3 a.m. night, go over hill and dale
and industrial park, over rail and trestles, into and out
of cities, beginning.

Day One

ℂℜ
... *Letters* ...

And the homeless man sits on the curb in the
parking lot wrapped in white blankets beside a stuffed
black trash bag --- 10 gallon size --- black hooded
sweat jersey pulled tight against light
rain, bustling commuters look past his perch, his
station: he is not there, he is not sitting on the curb
talking to himself, he is an unseen mumbling, a
scattering of sounds, almost a voice no head turns
toward. Early traffic creeps past stately brick homes,
cherry blossoms adorn sidewalks, swept along in light
winds, light rain, the morning
opens its full bloom.

Bridges appear unhinged at land's end, bridges in
fog, bridges in clouds bridge rivers, brown choppy
water sloshing to oceans, bridges, an act of faith.

In a blur meadow and marshland, wave of high
reeds, petroleum refinery, industry more gray in
lessening light, edge of the ocean and so much more
missed, moving rail and road, a cherry blossom
by another name.

Rain, wind, rain, wind and rain layered gray this
day closer to summer chilled by northern charms.

Haze on the half moon the night before the day
leaving the reservation, no moon or otherwise ending
this first night.

80
... Letters ...

Day Two

Soaked and what not soaked is beaded, an abundance of water, and a light mist, microdots of water in the air, but no wind the second day from the singular, wooded reservation.

Long Island, a drone of things moving, undercurrent of dysphonic sounds melt, a river of sounds, around islands of tulips on spindly stems clustered yellow, red, purple, pansies yellow, red, violet, pink banked below tulips purple, red, yellow, pansies and periwinkles blue pale blue on the hub of green lilies pattern embroiders scrubs, grass, young trees, buds tight and about to burst in the first bright sunlight.

And more showers and wind, now winds angling rain shaking scrubs, slender tree branches, and it's not warm on this edge of summer, here in this colder region.

One gull almost invisible in gray shifting sky screeches to the ocean, crows give chase.

Afternoon, late afternoon, a hazy sun, finally.

Bradford Pears drape sidewalks, white petals a scattered snow on red brick. Blackbirds, grackles, wrens, sparrows in out enormous rain water puddles, dipping fuzzy strands, shaking water, toss

CR
... Letters ...

and shake would be worms, hop off, gone to thick leaved trees. No wind, scintillating, radiant pansies, periwinkles, tulips, delight and cheer late afternoon light.

And then the dance of the man in white who smells of roses. Night was cold and no stars prevail.

Day Three

Hard wind. Rain. Dark gray sky southwest, pale gray northeast. Morning slow moving and heavy.

Later, shifting gray, rain. The only explosion mushroom clouds of white flowering pear trees over sidewalks and narrow lanes. Day
two puddles, lakes day three, no birds at the edges.

Summary: Direct quotes

"Fools are not suffered lightly. Polite is an add on. Service is pest control. Any big city is like that. Sometimes what is best for us is unknown to us. Suggest you get a t-shirt with:

I'm a really nice guy at heart
don't be rude to me

and have a large heart printed on it."

The last dance danced, the last cup of cheer

passed, brimming, passed and drained, and the man in white who smells of roses, gone out of the Temple, out of the city.

Postscript: Day After Day Three

Silence is deafening, stillness presents itself imposing and charismatic, the attraction overwhelming and profound. Azaleas in full flower
bent at the waist, only one bird chirps, occasionally. Every tree black, soaked in rain. Sedated sky one color blue-gray between high maples, oaks, hickory. Gray rock almost black and wet. No squirrels about this first morning settling into the rhythm of trees. Under this cloak of green leaves, inside my portable cave of solitude, I sit twigging a poem for you.

LETTER TO MY IMAGINARY WIFE
FROM OCTOBER

Early this crisp morning I walked the ravine southwest
beyond the flat breaking trail edging swampland
spongy and reed-braced. Sluggish water brown-black
and startling clear reflecting sunlight rising the low
hill behind me. It was calm under common oak and
pine, maple and hickory on the southeastern ridge.
Squirrels were undisturbed preparing for winter. Crows
and blackbirds squabbled branch to branch, tree to
tree ignoring me in their aggravation. I seemed to be
invisible, blended into the trees. My delight made time
elastic. And when my heart stopped, the world moved
at the speed of light. Such an exquisite, charming
moment bubbling in joy. I knew then every grain
of sand is numbered, there are no insignificant acts,
and the universe is a delicate balance we hold in our
hands. The soul is brighter than a thousand suns. Now
I can say to you, in October I heard God laughing in
a rainbow of leaves tumbling in the wind. Yes and
yes these colors are overwhelming, and even the light
sparkling off rocks is scintillating to a syllable. It is
easy in these woods to find the mystical force that
brought us together, keeps our connection immediate,
intimate, even at this distance, but my words are
disengaged, foreign things less interesting than drifting
leaves, swaying grass.   When I come to myself, I will
write.

ഇ
... Letters ...

THIS SIDE OF THE RIVER:
A LETTER TO MY IMAGINARY WIFE
FROM SCOTTSDALE, ARIZONA

Half moon late rising, clear stars across a wide sky.
December and the night has a chilly sting. A faint
trace of mountains, diaphanous bands of clouds drift,
widens. Stars are clear, but not many in this pale
night. This morning I watched a rabbit crouch under a
single scrub near the brush line. It stayed motionless
beside ostrich-egg shaped stones, blended the color
of sand, then vanished without disturbing the low
brush. I can't imagine what it is to be effortless, so
absent of a muddy water way of thinking that there is
no ripple when I act. On this side of the river the ten
thousand things wobble in my head like a drunken
man stumbling down the stairs. One misguided
moment (as the Zen Masters say) and the assorted
make-believes prance and play in my head without
end. Such entertainment is often interesting, and that
is my greatest folly. I can't seem to be spontaneous
as that rabbit moving through brush, and I know my
existence is equally troubled by dangers. I seem to be
more the laboring, questioning Job, than the ecstatic,
accepting St. Francis. This life is less than a moment
and gone. My snare is the question: On this side of the
river what really matters if everything is ephemeral, a
dream? I'm in love with my question: it's a comfort
like the stone the drowning man clings to as he sinks.
The high desert air holds no answers. I cannot fix my
direction by the stars. Can you teach me how to let go?

☙

... £etters ...

THE COLD END OF OCTOBER:
A LETTER FROM MY IMAGINARY WIFE

My love, we have shared pyrotechnical pleasures in
the past, danced those primitive dances that will not
warrant us Green Cards in heaven, but now I fear you
will think I have scales, a tail, and breathe fire. Wake
up Mackie. Get a life. Stop all this moping around
in the woods: it will turn your brain to mush. What
am I to do with your last grandiose ecstasy: "When
my heart stopped, the world moves at the speed of
light. Such an exquisite, charming moment bubbling
in joy" or your last hyperbole: "In October I heard
God laughing in a rainbow of leaves tumbling in
the wind." You may have realized every person you
encounter potentially holds the key to your spiritual
awakening, but I live in a fast place where people
talk on cell phones, dress smartly, walk briskly. Here
things are concrete, tangible. I can measure and judge
what happens about me. I cannot jumble this into that
metaphysical gibberish you wrote about Heisenberg's
"Uncertainty Theory," Kabala's shattered vessel
and all that giving and receiving light rubbish. You
may know, but I do not, that every act significant or
otherwise effects the balance of the Universe, and
that some small act of kindness may swing open the
locked doors of Eden. Sometimes, my love, I think
you have gone round the bend, gone schizie on me.
Are you hearing voices, seeing things that aren't there?
Should you get your medications adjusted? Have

you forgotten your mantra, "Better living through chemistry"? Please, my love, remember to breathe slowly, and repeat, "Better living through chemistry." I am, however, thankful you have not entwined yourself in all that "rapture" hocus-pocus peddled like packets of anthrax by that desiccated, hair-sprayed Jack Van Impe. Yes, there may be Universes within Universes, and the soul may be "Brighter than a thousand suns" as you have written, but I have to go with what I have here: right foot, left foot, down the stairs, down the road. It's nothing magical, infinitely practical. When you finish acting like Saint Frances of Assisi, chattering away at rocks, trees, and birds, write me.

POSTSCRIPT TO A LETTER:
TO MY IMAGINARY WIFE
FROM SCOTTSDALE, ARIZONA

Two weeks in the desert, thirsty, chilled at night under
bright stars, sweating in the morning sun,
I saw no flowers shimmering as your eyes everyday
you walked the dark, backwoods of Bowling Green.

... Letters ...

JANUARY BRIDE, JUNE HEART:
A LETTER FROM MY IMAGINARY WIFE

Since arriving in the city of gray cobblestone streets,
to toss myself into the fray for equality, to feed the
needy, and find shelter for the homeless; I've posh-
poshed your letters, pooh-poohed your poems, and
knocked about the stanza you often recited to me
walking woods replete with birdsongs:

Far from the maddening crowd's ignoble strife,
Their sober wishes never learned to stray;
Along the cool sequester'd vale of life
They kept the noiseless tenor of their way.

But rain, rain for a month, nothing but rain, rain. I'm
afloat, adrift in this aquatic realm, no landmarks on the
horizon to steer by, no clear sky to set my star chart.
Fancy, I once thought fancy a caution, a bollix at best;
however, long days, long nights in rain floated me into
and out of pretty pictures: a rescue from deeper waters.
Perhaps, I've attributed incorrectly qualities fancy
lends its practitioners. Here I flounder, I've fallen
into contractions, polysyllabic words, and complex
sentences: I'm confused and defended. Fancy
smoothes the waters. I've learned in my bath tub life
sloshing down those slick stones elbow to elbow with
the crowd that maddens.

A smiling Cheshire cat are you?
You've long known my defensive measures:

ভ
... Letters ...

contracting into myself, simultaneously propelling
outward linguistic sabers rattling. And you? Your
metaphysical twaddle, I've a notion, isn't loquacious
elegance, or jejune pap, or a claim to worlds within,
but your song, call "to retreat"
you've no inkling you sing as you circle up the
wagons. Are we two sea creatures in the same waters
equally swept by tides, equally learning to swim?
Cobblestone streets are hard, slippery when wet. We
can learn the ways of water. We can swim outside our
shells.

THE TROUBLE WITH WALKING:
A LETTER TO MY IMAGINARY WIFE

the trouble with walking
CM

                                     I walked
city streets, walked white-gray concrete cracked and
worn, walked past storefront and house windows
barred in black jail bars, walked past men and women
of every nation speaking melodic languages drudging
along the white-gray walkway.
                            I walked the high desert,
walked in swirling dust scooting through sage and
cactus, pushing tumbleweeds, heat waves altering
the light down the trail bleached bone dry under one
enormous blue sky.
                          In the forest, the first sunny
day in a month, the air green-pea-soup, that wet and
thick. Everywhere green has exploded in rippling
green and shadow. Rocks, gray granite rocks banked
up bracing the earthen wall, look denser, deeper in
depth, if stone has a depth. A black ribbon slithers
along so quickly it seems an illusion, a trick of the eye,
but the black snake is quick in the open below where
oaks are two years, three years up from acorns.
                        Wind moves a little and low. Sunlight
catches spider webs and lines of light pattern the
air between bushes, a moment, and gone. Broad
leaves on little hickory trees flap like elephant ears
in rising wind, and a pox on those deerflies, a plague

on their brother horseflies: nibblers and biters both. One hummingbird streaks around, then suddenly there hovering [the ultimate art of the paradox, the conundrum of motionless flight].

Fuzzy impulse-driven fur-balled squirrels absolutely mad in season dart through passages in the underbrush, shake those elephant ears to rattling pursing their passion. This is a busy place. Did I mention carpenter bees droning or those tank-like black ants? Clouds cross the sun out and this place folds into another dimension, a secret world in half-light. Crazy as it seems, the wind stops when clouds darken the woods. Nothing moves. The forest appears to hold its breath, but high above in maples, one woodpecker glides to a large oak, and bird songs begin. There is one dragonfly doing yoga on the azalea, [stretch, snap back, stretch] those long paddle wings are the top part of [!] in glossy black-silk. Earth rain soaked sucks at my footprints, squished marks on last year's leaves. I make no sound walking, no wet squiggle the spongy forest wiggles back and flat and leaves no sign of my passing. Eternally, I am your walking wind.

RAGTIME
THROWING THE BONES:
A LETTER FROM MY IMAGINARY WIFE

The beer guzzlers are dead quiet this morning, their
night terrorizing this neighborhood only a pleasantly
dull dream to them now. Sunday morning in the city
of cobblestone streets. One or two joggers huffing,
puffing the best city air, an elderly man and woman
walk a small dab of white dog, and are simply an
actual representation of the phrase: "slow as molasses
in January." They are a marvel to watch, to observe
how the smallest movement is years of understanding
crystallized, coded, and conveyed with complete
assurance each knows exactly what the other means.
It is not telepathy, but as close as human existence
allows, confined as we are in our individual prisons
or dungeons, depending on our temperament. I write
in the first person pleural, how manly of me. I have
given up some of my graces to walk hard stones of
this city, to pull up my britches (one leg at a time)
for the food kitchen, the homeless shelter, daycare
for single mothers, English language classes for new
arrivals to our country, and to march the streets waving
my banner to end the meanness to brown women and
men up from South America. And with the graces
goes patience, now replaced by frustration with the
uncharming side of the phrase, "slow as molasses in
January" social change. That haunts me daily. Does
kindness take a lifetime to learn? Can't common
courtesy become part of our DNA? And then there is

Earl Gray tea and the Sunday paper. Mogadishu, home
of pirates roving the high sea (a curious occupation for
a desert country). Somalia, what to do with Somalia,
a country whose only industry is war on land and
sea. Car bombs and body counts in Iraq, Pakistan,
Afghanistan.
Wounded & dead presented like scores from a cricket
match. And there is the bobbing account of the Stock
Market and oil prices, both tethered to peace/tension in
the Middle East.

North Korea ignores United Nation Security
Counsel warning and set off an underground nuclear
test, launches mid & long range missiles sailing
into the sea (not at pirates). Nervous Russia, Japan,
and South Korea are calling for more international
sanctions against North Korea. And the North
Korean people continue to starve, prisoners of their
government.

Closer to home: Michael Vick, recently released
from prison, will do his community service work
with the Humane Society. He will be a spokes person
against dog fighting. Some "jaded"
critics believe his angle is to appease the NFL enough
to get back in the game where the money is good.
But it is not all bleak and dreary.

On a bright, brighter, brightest note: a brown
woman, a Hispanic woman, diligent and talented, (no
silver spoon anywhere near the neighborhood where

she was raised) is now up for confirmation to the
Supreme Court of the United States of America. Can
it be more hopeful for this country? Can I be more
revitalized?

I guess those molasses are moving along, January
in the heart heating up more than I first considered
& maybe those old molasses will get to the pancakes
while they are still warm, while we are young
enough to taste them. Perhaps my graces are not
actually gone, or gone so far I cannot call them home.

Sunday morning. The wind has stopped its week of
tossing trees about, and this rain beginning, small and
gentle, is your rain as well.

... *Letters* ...

CR
... Letters ...